# RUST ON THE SAW TEETH

## Thomas Tilton

**Rust on the Saw Teeth**

First Printing

ISBN  978-1-970860-00-9

Cover Art Credit: Katsushika Hokusai. Kohada Koheiji, from the series "One Hundred Ghost Tales (Hyaku monogatari)," 1931-1932. The Art Institute of Chicago.

**CUTTLEFISH
BOOKS**

# RUST ON THE SAW TEETH

silencing
the screaming hordes
music box

two coins
over the dead man's eyes
flutter

costume party
the cadavers
a little too lifelike

monochrome monsters
across the basement windows
a splash of red

incantation...
a dragon escapes
the bestiary

vacancy
at the charnel house
renters swarm

metal to metal
the clink
of the iron maiden

the shrill cry
of past tenants
forever home

casting spells
the witch's splayed
tongue

his effigy
holding her place
in the grimoire

rapt...
the gorgon
tucking a strand

only scratching
the surface
cat o'nine tails

hour of the wolf
I blow my breath
at the moon

faint traces
of her familiar's song
a low yowl

ghost house
an old bow rake
propping the fence

Hand of Glory
at a crossroads
at a standstill

cutting a slit
through the fog
nightwalker

in the shadows
she's something else
puma

stage whisper
he tells them
what's in store

billowing sails
in the doldrums
a ghost ship changes course

settling sounds
the old house
never lost a tenant

he has his
mother's face
shadow box

her fingers tracing
the looking glass—
ripples

the half-moon
curve of his forelock
wolf den

showing off
her cross-stitching
sutures

lovers' lane
her hook
in my hand

make-out point
she barely escapes
the asylum

garrote
the piano always
out of tune

moonshine
the wolf looking back
at me

after the seance
the tea pouring
itself

campsite...
a crackling fire
drowns out the footfalls

wading the river
my toes brush something
coiled

moonset
a tail swishing
the fog

hickeys...
she attaches another
leech

rust on the saw teeth
the fix-it man's gleaming
smile

cutting eyeholes
in a burlap sack
the reaper

long pig
the butcher wipes his brow
with a forearm

flotsam
the doll's eyes open
and shut

candlelit supper
the spaghetti slurp
of a rat's tail

smoldering
she tosses his wax effigy
on the fire

children's wing—
the pitter-patter
of cloven feet

cutting the thread
with her teeth
no more wandering eyes

aiming for her heart
the knife thrower
blows a kiss

lean times
the undertaker
palms a crown

wolf sightings
she pulls the strings
on her red hoodie

nights eternal
sipping from the same
wound

cloud wisps
across a thumbnail
eldritch moon

hall of mirrors
each one shaping
a new face

# ABOUT THE AUTHOR

Thomas Tilton is the founding editor of the horror senryu journal, an online journal of horror-themed haiku and senryu at horrorkujournal.blogspot.com. His previous chapbook, *Paper Houses*, is available through Amazon. He lives in Michigan.

www.ingramcontent.com/pod-product-compliance
Lightning Source LLC
Chambersburg PA
CBHW051243120626
46547CB00014B/1776